WELCOME

Thank you for choosing to walk this path with me. You hold in your hands more than a journal — you hold a sacred space for your healing journey.

This companion journal was thoughtfully created as a hand-in-hand partner to Holding Without Breaking: A Guide to Navigating Grief, Setting Boundaries, and Finding Strength — How Adult Children Can Support a Grieving Parent Without Losing Themselves.

If you've discovered this journal on its own, I gently encourage you to explore the main book as well. The reflections and prompts within these pages are direct extensions of the book's heart and teachings — crafted to deepen your understanding, connection, and personal renewal.

Together, the book and journal offer a complete journey of awareness, compassion, and grace — helping you navigate the tender balance between holding and healing.

As you begin this sacred work, may you move at your own pace, rest when needed, and remember that healing isn't about perfection — it's about presence. This journal is your personal sanctuary: a place to write, to release, and to remember that your story still matters.

DEDICATION

Inspired by my mother, Delores, whose quiet strength reminds me that even after profound loss, love still finds a way to bloom—and that true resilience often comes in the gentlest of steps.

To all who are holding everything together while feeling like they're falling apart.

To every adult child supporting a grieving parent while carrying their own sorrow — this space sees you.

Your strength is undeniable. Your love is felt. And your unseen pain is profoundly acknowledged.

This journal is your steady companion.

You are not alone.

Note from the Author

As I moved through my own journey of grief and caregiving — with its unspoken burdens, unexpected turns, and quiet moments of self-discovery — I often longed for a space to breathe, to process, to simply be.

This journal is that space.

Born from lived experience and deep reflection, it is my heartfelt offering to you — a gentle companion for the days that feel heavy, and for the moments that remind you of your own strength.

May it hold you tenderly as you walk your own path of holding without breaking.

— Mischere

How To Use
This Journal

This is your space — and there's no single "right" way to use it.

Synchronized Reflection
Pair your reading of Holding Without Breaking with this journal. After each chapter, turn to the matching section here to engage more deeply with its themes and prompts. Let the pages become a dialogue between the book, your heart, and your healing.

Organic Processing
Keep this journal nearby as you read or move through your days. When a passage stirs something tender, pause. Breathe. Write what surfaces — a single thought, a scattered fragment, or a full page of release. Let your words be honest, not polished.

Honesty & Openness
This is a judgment-free space. Write as much or as little as you need, in whatever form feels most true — lists, letters, prayers, reflections, or quiet notes that help you steady your breath. These pages exist solely for your growth and restoration.

Use the prompts ahead as gentle invitations to:
- Pause and acknowledge your own grief.
- Explore the shifting dynamics within your family.
- Plan tangible steps for self-care and boundary-setting.
- Unpack the unseen weights you carry.
- Celebrate your moments of resilience, grace, and renewal.

This is your journey of holding without breaking — one brave, imperfect step at a time.

Before You Begin

Before you turn the page, take a slow, steady breath.

You've already done something brave — you've chosen to face what hurts with honesty instead of avoidance. This journal isn't about finding the perfect words. It's about giving your truth a place to land.
Grief is not linear. Some days you may have paragraphs pouring out of you. Other days, a single word might be all you can manage — and that, too, is enough.

Let this be a space where time slows down, where you can lay down the weight of needing to hold it all together. There is no right pace, no right order, no wrong way to begin. Only the act of showing up — tenderly, truthfully, and without judgment.

Before you begin writing, take a moment to center yourself:
- Breathe in deeply, and exhale what no longer serves you.
- Whisper gratitude for the love that shaped you.
- Invite grace into the parts of you that still ache.

Then, if it feels right, respond to one or two of these reflections to help you arrive on the page:

- *Today, I give myself permission to…*
- *When I think about holding without breaking, I want to remember…*
- *Right now, my heart feels…*
- *If these pages could hold anything for me, I hope they hold…*

Wherever you begin, begin *gently.*

Your healing has already started — the moment you picked up this pen.

> "
You're not here to break. You're here to rise... slowly, gently, fiercely if you must. One breath. One boundary. One step at a time.

A Note Before The Work

You've arrived at the edge of beginning — not just of this journal, but of your own unfolding.

Before you move into Part One, pause here.
Breathe. Feel the ground beneath you.
This is the space between preparation and practice — where you turn inward and decide what this journey will mean for you.

You don't need to have the right words.
You don't need to be "ready."
You only need to be willing — to meet yourself with honesty, grace, and gentleness.

Let this be the page where you name your intention for what's ahead.

What do you hope to release, understand, or reclaim through this process?
What part of your story is ready to be seen or softened?

Take a few moments to write from the heart.

There's no wrong way to begin — only the act of showing up matters

MY REFLECTION BEFORE I BEGIN:

(Use this space to write freely. You might start with one of these prompts:)
- Today, I am choosing to begin because…
- What I hope this journal helps me uncover is…
- The part of my heart that needs the most care right now is…
- My intention for this season of healing is…

_____

_____

_____

_____

_____

_____

_____

_____

_____

_____

_____

_____

_____

_____

_____

_____

_____

_____

_____

_____

_____

_____

_____

_____

NOTES & REFLECTIONS

PART I

The Wave & The Weight

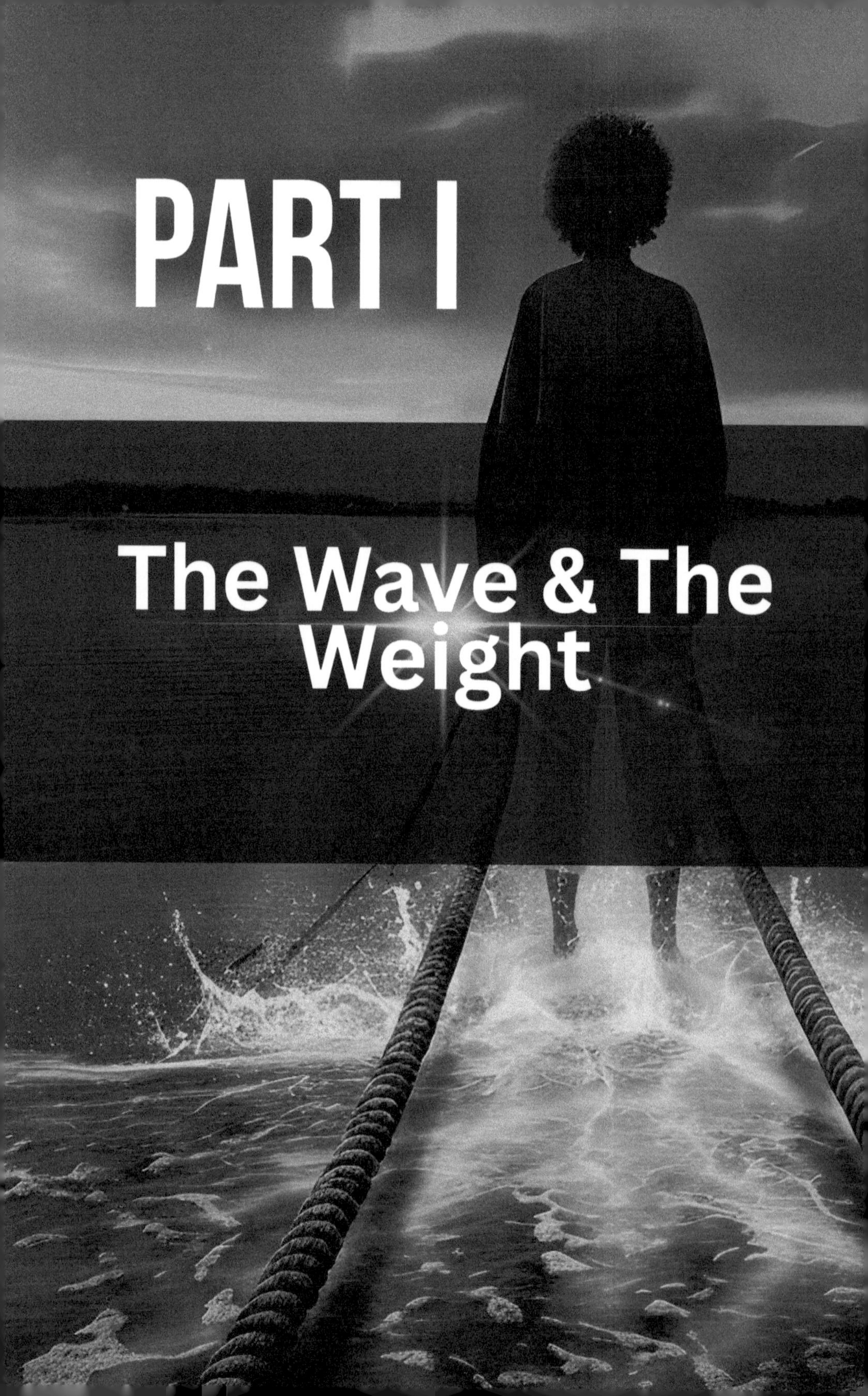

Chapter 1
When the Wave Hits

Chapter 1

These aren't puzzles to solve—they're gentle invitations. Each question opens a space for your grief to speak, in a season when so much feels fragile and uncertain.

Which responsibility am I carrying that doesn't truly belong to me?

_____

_____

_____

_____

_____

_____

What is one small task I could release—even if it feels uncomfortable—to make space for my own healing?

_____

_____

_____

_____

_____

_____

When have I worn the mask of "the strong one" while secretly breaking inside?

_____

_____

_____

_____

Chapter 1

If my grief had a sound—would it be silence, a sob, a scream, or something softer?

_____

_____

_____

_____

_____

_____

_____

What single, concrete act of care would help me

_____

_____

_____

_____

_____

_____

_____

If I could tell _one safe person_ the unedited truth, what would I say?

_____

_____

_____

_____

_____

_____

_____

_____

NOTES & REFLECTIONS

Practical Anchors for the First Wave

- **Assign a Point Person** – Let one trusted person handle updates so you're not reliving the shock with every call. After losing my stepfather, I asked one of my sisters to tell the others. That choice gave me a moment to breathe.
- **Ground Yourself in the Smallest Tasks**– Pour a glass of water. Put both feet on the floor. Name three things you can see and touch.
- **Accept Help You Didn't Plan For** – When someone offers to drive, cook, or make a call, say yes.
- **Let Silence Be Your Shield**– You don't have to pick up every call or text. Silence isn't selfish—it's space to breathe.
- **Do / Delegate / Drop**– Make a three-column list. Keep only what truly needs you. Ask one person to own the delegate column for a week.

Notes 2
REMEMBER

CLOSING THOUGHT

Grief folds you into new shapes. It teaches the weight of love and the fragility of life.

In those first moments, you may feel hollow. Lost. Like a part of you left with them.

But you are still here. Still breathing. And that, in itself, is strength. This journey is not about holding everything together perfectly. It is about moving forward with courage, even when the ground feels unsteady.

The wave will crash. The weight will press. But you are not here to break. You are here to rise—slowly, gently, fiercely if you must. One breath. One boundary. One step at a time.

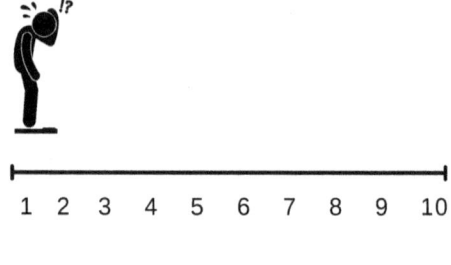

A Self-Check Scale

The Unseen Weight: On a scale of 1 to 10, where would you place yourself on the balance of carrying your own grief versus your parent's?

1 2 3 4 5 6 7 8 9 10

1: *I am actively holding space for my own grief while supporting my parent, and I feel a sense of emotional balance.*
10: *I feel completely consumed by my parent's grief, and my own feels heavy and invisible.*

My number today is: _____

Quite
REFLECTION

What emotion has been the loudest for you today

_____
_____
_____
_____
_____
_____
_____
_____
_____

What detail _____
about your loved _____
one surfaced _____
today—a sound, _____
a phrase, a
habit? _____

How did you show yourself grace, even in a small way?

_____
_____
_____
_____
_____
_____
_____
_____

NOTES & REFLECTIONS

NOTES & REFLECTIONS

Daily Check In

MOOD ☺ ☹ 😐 😲 ☹

WEATHER ☀ ☁ 🌬 🌧 ❄

DATE : _____

M T W T F S S

TODAY I FEEL

TODAY'S AFFIRMATION

- ●
- ●
- ●
- ●
- ●

TODAY'S MANTRA

TODAY I'M PROUD OF

- ●
- ●
- ●
- ●
- ●

TODAY'S MEMORY I CHOOSE TO CHERISH

TODAY'S GOAL

- ●
- ●
- ●
- ●
- ●

OPEN NOTES

TOMORROW'S PLAN

- ●
- ●
- ●
- ●

Chapter 2
The Undertow of Always Doing

> **The early days after loss are heavy. Not just with what's been taken, but with what's suddenly placed in your hands.**

Chapter 2

These aren't answers you must chase—they're gentle invitations. Each question gives you a way to sit with what changed the moment the news came, and how you are still carrying it now.

Where was I when the news came, and how has that place changed for me since?

_____

_____

_____

_____

_____

_____

_____

What is one detail from that day that still lingers most vividly in my mind?

_____

_____

_____

_____

_____

_____

_____

In what ways did time feel like it fractured—before and after?

_____

_____

_____

_____

_____

_____

Chapter 2 CONT.

If I could name the emotion beneath the shock, what would it be?

_____

_____

_____

_____

_____

_____

_____

How did I step into action, and what did that reveal about me?

_____

_____

_____

_____

_____

_____

Your answers may soften or sharpen over time. That shifting is part of grief's rhythm. May these questions hold you steady as you breathe through the memory.

CREATIVE SPACE

Practical Anchors for
the Undertow

- **Share the Updates Load –** Instead of fielding every "How's your mom, or dad?" call, set up a group text or rotate check-ins with siblings or cousins. Even that small handoff lightens the undertow.
- **Block Grief Breaks –** Step away, even briefly. Sit in silence, sip tea, or walk outside—remind your body it still deserves rest.
- **Let Them Reclaim Tasks –** Invite your parent back into small responsibilities when they're ready. Even folding laundry or paying a bill restores dignity.
- **Ask for Specific Help –** Replace vague offers like "Let me know if you need anything" with one concrete ask: "Could you bring dinner Wednesday night?" Clear asks, create clear support.
- **Track Your Emotional Temperature –** End each day with a pause: Did I feel my own grief today? If the answer is "no" for too many days, it's time to slow down and listen inward.

Notes 2
REMEMBER

NOTES & REFLECTIONS

CLOSING THOUGHT

Busyness may shield you for a time, but it cannot carry you forever. Tasks end. Papers get filed. Lists get crossed off. And when the silence returns, grief is still there, waiting to be felt.

You don't have to disappear in your parent's grief—or in your own tasks—to prove your love. Your healing matters too.

This isn't selfishness—it's survival.
One pause. One boundary. One honest answer to the question: How am I holding up today?

Because strength isn't in doing everything. It's in daring to take the mask off and letting yourself be seen—messy, human, grieving, and still worthy of care.

A Self-Check Scale

The Unseen Weight: On a scale of 1 to 10, where would you place yourself on the balance of carrying your own grief versus your parent's?

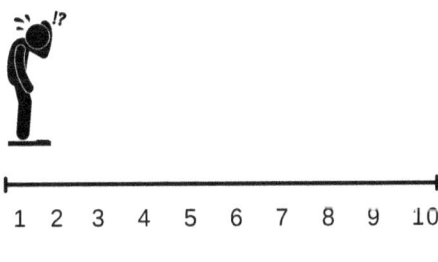

1 2 3 4 5 6 7 8 9 10

1: *I am actively holding space for my own grief while supporting my parent, and I feel a sense of emotional balance.*
10: *I feel completely consumed by my parent's grief, and my own feels heavy and invisible.*

My number today is: _____

Quite
REFLECTION

What emotion has been the loudest for you today

_____
_____
_____
_____
_____
_____
_____
_____
_____

What detail   _____
about your loved   _____
one surfaced
today—a sound,   _____
a phrase, a   _____
habit?   _____

How did you show yourself grace, even in a small way?

_____
_____
_____
_____
_____
_____
_____
_____

NOTES & REFLECTIONS

Daily Check In

MOOD ☺ ☹ 😐 😵 😣

WEATHER ☀ ☁ 💨 🌧 ❄

DATE : _____

M T W T F S S

TODAY I FEEL

TODAY'S AFFIRMATION

-
-
-
-
-

TODAY'S MANTRA

TODAY I'M PROUD OF

-
-
-
-
-

TODAY'S MEMORY I CHOOSE TO CHERISH

TODAY'S GOAL

-
-
-
-
-

OPEN NOTES

TOMORROW'S PLAN

-
-
-
-

Chapter 3
When Holding on Holds You Back

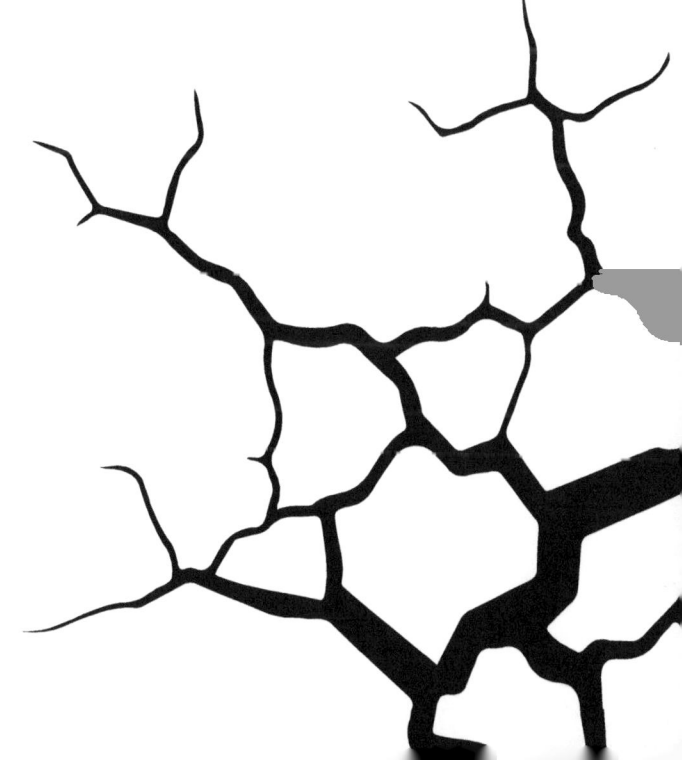

66

Sometimes the best way to help is to step aside and let them try.
- Unknown

Chapter 3

These aren't puzzles to solve—they're invitations. Each question gives you space to notice the difference between helping that heals and helping that hinders.

Take a slow breath. Let your shoulders soften. When you're ready, allow these questions to meet you where you are:

When have I stepped in for my parent without asking if they wanted help?

_____

_____

_____

_____

_____

_____

_____

What task or ritual might actually strengthen my parent's sense of independence if I let them keep it?

_____

_____

_____

_____

_____

_____

_____

What was I afraid would happen if I stepped back?

_____

_____

_____

_____

Chapter 3 CONT.

How do my siblings or family members express their love through "help," and how is it different from mine?

_____

_____

_____

_____

_____

_____

_____

_____

What would it look like to offer both freedom and backup—the reassurance that my parent is not alone, even when they choose to do something themselves?

_____

_____

_____

_____

_____

_____

Your answers may shift over time, just as roles shift. That's not failure—it's growth. May these questions remind you that stepping back can be as loving as stepping in.

_____

_____

_____

_____

NOTES & REFLECTIONS

BONUS ACTIVITY
Redefining Help

Sometimes "helping" becomes our way of holding on.
This exercise invites you to redefine what helping means now that the first chaos has passed.

Reflect and write:
- What did you believe your parent needed most in those early days of grief?
- What do you see now that they actually needed — or that you needed?
- Finish this sentence:

Helping now means: _____
(Use this redefinition as a touchstone whenever you feel pulled to over-hold or over-carry.)

_____

_____

_____

_____

_____

_____

_____

_____

_____

_____

_____

Closing Thought
Sometimes, the hardest part of helping is learning when to let go.
Your care is not measured by how much you do, but by the compassion you carry — for them and for yourself.

NOTES & REFLECTIONS

THREE

CLOSING THOUGHT

Grief asks a lot of us, but it never asked for perfection.

Sometimes, the most courageous thing you can do is release the rope—trusting that others can and will step in. Because the moment you loosen your grip, you create space for something surprising to happen:

They rise.
You breathe.
And the tide feels just a little less heavy.

Loosening my grip didn't mean walking away—it meant walking beside her differently. And as I began to see, grief wasn't only changing her routines. It was reshaping the woman I had always known.

A Self-Check Scale

The Unseen Weight: On a scale of 1 to 10, where would you place yourself on the balance of carrying your own grief versus your parent's?

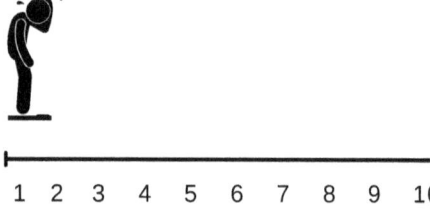

1 2 3 4 5 6 7 8 9 10

1: *I am actively holding space for my own grief while supporting my parent, and I feel a sense of emotional balance.*
10: *I feel completely consumed by my parent's grief, and my own feels heavy and invisible.*

My number today is: _____

Quite
REFLECTION

What emotion has been the loudest for you today

_____
_____
_____
_____
_____
_____
_____
_____
_____

What detail about your loved one surfaced today—a sound, a phrase, a habit?

_____
_____
_____
_____
_____

How did you show yourself grace, even in a small way?

_____
_____
_____
_____
_____
_____
_____
_____

NOTES & REFLECTIONS

Daily Check In

MOOD   😊 😟 😑 😵 😣

WEATHER   ☀️ ☁️ 💨 🌧️ ❄️

DATE : _____

M   T   W   T   F   S   S

TODAY I FEEL

TODAY'S AFFIRMATION

-
-
-
-
-

TODAY'S MANTRA

TODAY I'M PROUD OF

-
-
-
-
-

TODAY'S MEMORY I CHOOSE TO CHERISH

TODAY'S GOAL

-
-
-
-
-

OPEN NOTES

TOMORROW'S PLAN

-
-
-
-

Chapter 4

The Quiet Shift You Don't See Coming

"

The death of a spouse doesn't just break your parent's heart—it reshapes their identity. And sometimes, that shift reshapes yours too.

Chapter 4

When I paused to look inward, I realized the shift wasn't only hers—it was mine too. You may find the same.

How has my parent shifted since the loss—and how have I?

_____

_____

_____

_____

_____

_____

_____

What part of them am I holding onto that may never fully return?

_____

_____

_____

_____

_____

_____

_____

Where can I steady with firmer boundaries—or soften with deeper compassion—so we both keep balance?

_____

_____

_____

_____

_____

_____

Chapter 4 CONT.

These aren't demands for answers. They're gentle mirrors. Each question opens a space to see both your parent and yourself more clearly—as you are now, not as you once were.

What rituals, no matter how small, still tether us to connection?

_____

_____

_____

_____

_____

_____

_____

THE INVISIBLE QUESTION:

Think back to a time when someone asked how you were—but not how you really were.
What was the answer you held back? What truth sat quietly beneath your smile?

_____

_____

_____

_____

_____

_____

_____

_____

_____

_____

_____

_____

Practical Anchors for
Navigating the Quiet Shift

- **Name the Change Without Blame:** A gentle, "I've noticed you've been quieter lately—how are you feeling?" created room for honesty without shame.

- **Preserve Small Rituals:** Even scaled-back traditions carried power. Brewing coffee and sitting with her for ten quiet minutes each morning became our new anchor.

- **Balance the Roles:** Writing down what she once managed and what I now carried helped me see where I could hand back small responsibilities when she was ready.

- **Honor the Pause:** Long silences didn't mean failure. They meant processing.

- **Invite Their Wisdom Back In:** Even fragile, our parents still hold lifetimes of insight. Asking for her advice—on a recipe, a memory, even a family story—restored dignity and reminded her she was more than her grief.

Notes 2
REMEMBER

NOTES & REFLECTIONS

FOUR

CLOSING THOUGHT

Grief reshapes two lives at once.

Your parent may never return to who they were before, and you may never return to who you were before. But that doesn't mean love has disappeared. It means both of you are slowly learning how to meet each other again—awkwardly, tenderly, in this new terrain.

Patience becomes the bridge. Every small ritual kept, every pause honored, every moment you choose compassion over correction creates space for transformation—space for your parent to rebuild and for you to breathe.

The quiet shift isn't about replacing what was lost. It's about discovering who you both are now—and how love still lives here. One step. One pause. One fragile, surprising laugh at a time.

A Self-Check Scale

The Unseen Weight: On a scale of 1 to 10, where would you place yourself on the balance of carrying your own grief versus your parent's?

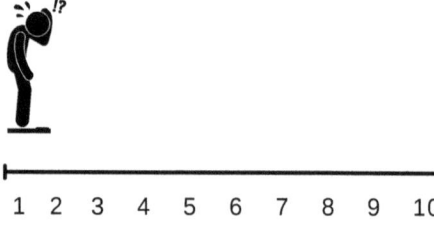

1 2 3 4 5 6 7 8 9 10

1: *I am actively holding space for my own grief while supporting my parent, and I feel a sense of emotional balance.*
10: *I feel completely consumed by my parent's grief, and my own feels heavy and invisible.*

My number today is: _____

Quite REFLECTION

What emotion has been the loudest for you today

_____
_____
_____
_____
_____
_____
_____
_____
_____

What detail about your loved one surfaced today—a sound, a phrase, a habit?

_____
_____
_____
_____
_____

How did you show yourself grace, even in a small way?

_____
_____
_____
_____
_____
_____
_____
_____

NOTES & REFLECTIONS

Daily Check In

MOOD ☺ ☹ 😐 😵 😣

WEATHER ☀ ☁ 🌬 🌧 ❄

DATE : _____

M T W T F S S

TODAY I FEEL

TODAY'S AFFIRMATION

-
-
-
-
-

TODAY'S MANTRA

TODAY I'M PROUD OF

-
-
-
-
-

TODAY'S MEMORY I CHOOSE TO CHERISH

TODAY'S GOAL

-
-
-
-
-

OPEN NOTES

TOMORROW'S PLAN

-
-
-
-

Chapter 5
When Joy Feels Like Betrayal

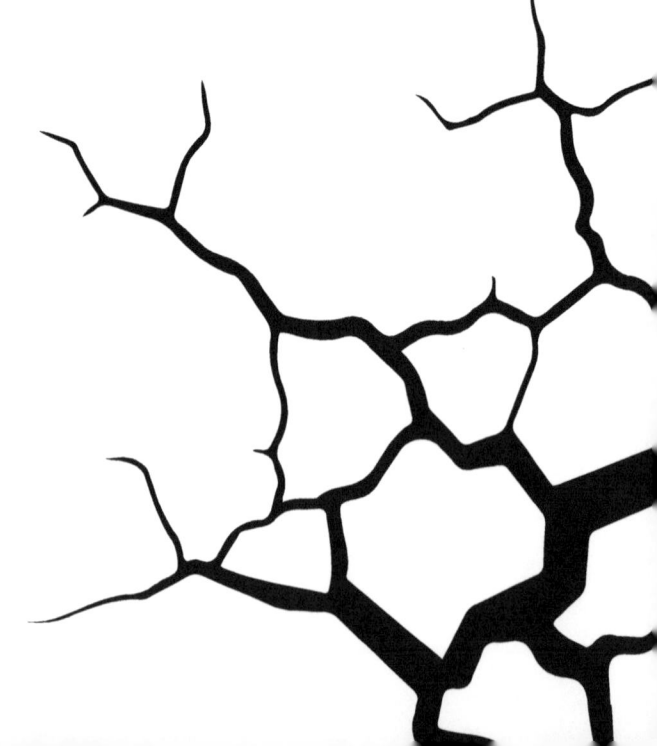

66

When someone you love dies, it feels wrong to keep living. But healing doesn't dishonor them– it honors you both.

Chapter 5

Exhale slowly. Notice where joy feels heavy in your body, like a stone you're not sure you should lift.

What ordinary joy have I felt guilty for reaching toward?

_____

_____

_____

_____

_____

_____

_____

Where could I welcome grace back in—without apology, without shame?

_____

_____

_____

_____

_____

_____

_____

How might I carry their memory into joy, like a current moving alongside me rather than against me?

_____

_____

_____

_____

_____

Chapter 5 CONT.

Who in my circle could remind me that joy is not disloyalty but resilience?

_____
_____
_____
_____
_____
_____
_____
_____
_____
_____

What small joy feels safe enough to practice this week?

_____
_____
_____
_____
_____
_____
_____
_____
_____
_____
_____
_____

NOTES & REFLECTIONS

Practical Anchors:
Inviting Joy Back In

- **Start Small** – A walk in the park. A favorite meal. Something low-stakes that feels doable.

- **Blend Joy with Memory – Order their favorite dessert. Play their favorite '70s track while cooking. Let their presence be part of the moment.**

- **Set a Gentle Boundary** – If it feels overwhelming, give the activity a time frame. "I'll stay for an hour" can take the pressure off.

- **Name the Guilt** – If it surfaces, ask: Is this guilt mine, or is it tied to what I think others expect of me?

- **Reflect Afterwards** – Journal or voice-note the emotions that came up. No judgment, just witness.

- **Share Joy Out Loud** – Tell someone close, "I laughed today—and it felt strange." Naming it helps normalize it.

Notes 2
REMEMBER

CLOSING THOUGHT

Grief is a long road. But joy is not betrayal—it's survival. Let yourself return to life gently.

You're not leaving them behind. You're learning how to carry them forward.

Each laugh. Each breath. Each small joy is not a betrayal— it's proof you're still carrying them with you.

And yet, as you let life back in, another truth emerges: not every gesture of comfort comforts. Some words meant to encourage land like dismissal. Some offers of help press heavier than the grief itself.

Learning to navigate those moments is part of the work too.

A Self-Check Scale

The Unseen Weight: On a scale of 1 to 10, where would you place yourself on the balance of carrying your own grief versus your parent's?

1 2 3 4 5 6 7 8 9 10

1: *I am actively holding space for my own grief while supporting my parent, and I feel a sense of emotional balance.* **10:** *I feel completely consumed by my parent's grief, and my own feels heavy and invisible.*

My number today is: _____

Quite
REFLECTION

What emotion has been the loudest for you today

_____
_____
_____
_____
_____
_____
_____
_____
_____

What detail about your loved one surfaced today—a sound, a phrase, a habit?

_____
_____
_____
_____

How did you show yourself grace, even in a small way?

_____
_____
_____
_____
_____
_____
_____
_____

NOTES & REFLECTIONS

Daily Check In

MOOD   😊 😞 😐 😵 😣

WEATHER   ☀ ☁ 🌬 🌧 ❄

DATE : _____

M T W T F S S

TODAY I FEEL

TODAY'S AFFIRMATION

-
-
-
-
-

TODAY'S MANTRA

TODAY I'M PROUD OF

-
-
-
-
-

TODAY'S MEMORY I CHOOSE TO CHERISH

TODAY'S GOAL

-
-
-
-
-

OPEN NOTES

TOMORROW'S PLAN

-
-
-
-

Chapter 6
When the Help Isn't Helping

Support is only helpful when it honors your reality—not when it adds to your burden.

Chapter 6

Pause. Picture the last time someone offered help. Feel into your body: did it lighten you, or weigh you down?

What kind of support feels like a lifeline—and what drags me under?

_____

_____

_____

_____

_____

_____

_____

Where have I accepted "help" that left me emptier instead of steadier?

_____

_____

_____

_____

_____

_____

_____

_____

_____

_____

_____

_____

Chapter 6 CONT.

What support do I long for but haven't found the courage to
ask for?

_____

_____

_____

_____

_____

_____

_____

_____

Where have I confused gratitude with obligation?

_____

_____

_____

_____

_____

_____

_____

How can I name the help that steadies me, like an oar
keeping me in rhythm with the waves?

_____

_____

_____

_____

_____

_____

Chapter 6

Reach-Out Reflection: Learning to Ask for Help
It's okay to need help.

Grief often convinces us we should manage everything alone—but healing asks for community.

This exercise helps you name the small and specific ways others can step in, so you can breathe a little easier.

Prompt:
List three specific things you could use help with right now—big or small. It might be picking up groceries, making a few phone calls, or spending time with your parent so you can rest.
Think of this as your reach-out list—tasks you'll intentionally share with family or friends instead of carrying alone.

_____

_____

_____

_____

_____

_____

_____

_____

_____

NOTES & REFLECTIONS

CLOSING THOUGHT

From pies at the door, to words that stung on the road, to calls that left me weary, I learned this: not all help helps.

And naming that doesn't make you ungrateful—it makes you honest. You deserve support that sustains you, not drains you.

Support that meets you where you are, not where someone else thinks you should be.

One boundary. One breath. One true connection at a time.

CREATIVE SPACE

Quite REFLECTION

What emotion has been the loudest for you today

_____

_____

_____

_____

_____

_____

_____

_____

What detail about your loved one surfaced today—a sound, a phrase, a habit?

_____

_____

_____

_____

_____

How did you show yourself grace, even in a small way?

_____

_____

_____

_____

_____

_____

_____

_____

NOTES & REFLECTIONS

Daily Check In

MOOD   ☺ ☹ 😑 😵 😕

WEATHER   ☀ ☁ 🌬 🌧 ❄

DATE : _____

M   T   W   T   F   S   S

TODAY I FEEL

TODAY'S AFFIRMATION
-
-
-
-
-

TODAY'S MANTRA

TODAY I'M PROUD OF
-
-
-
-
-

TODAY'S MEMORY I CHOOSE TO CHERISH

TODAY'S GOAL
-
-
-
-
-

OPEN NOTES

TOMORROW'S PLAN
-
-
-
-

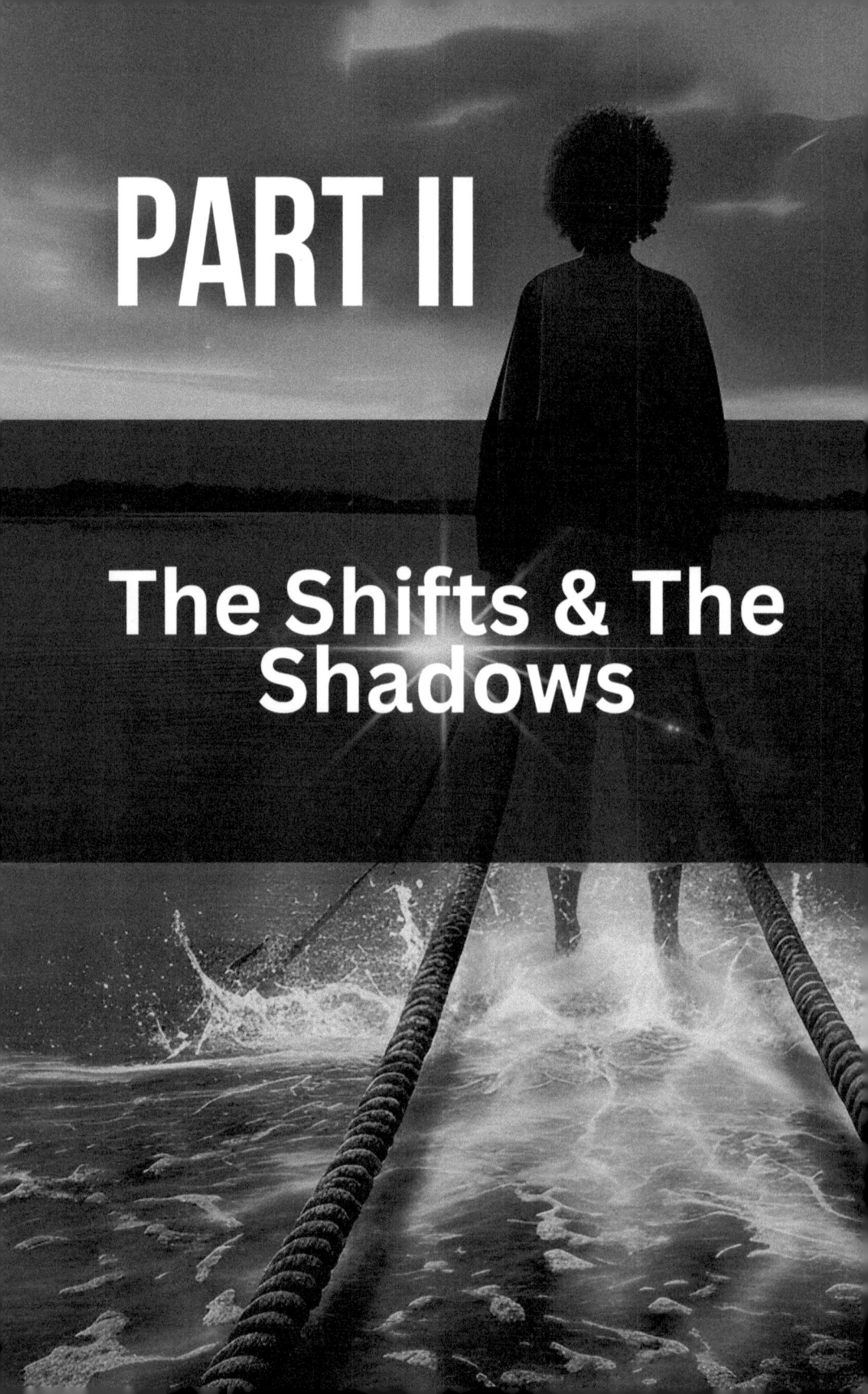

PART II

The Shifts & The Shadows

NOTES & REFLECTIONS

NOTES & REFLECTIONS

Daily Check In

MOOD   😊 😞 😑 😵 😣

WEATHER   ☀ ☁ 💨 🌧 ❄

DATE : _____

M T W T F S S

TODAY I FEEL

TODAY'S MANTRA

TODAY'S MEMORY I CHOOSE TO CHERISH

OPEN NOTES

TODAY'S AFFIRMATION

-
-
-
-
-

TODAY I'M PROUD OF

-
-
-
-
-

TODAY'S GOAL

-
-
-
-
-

TOMORROW'S PLAN

-
-
-
-

Chapter 7
Time Doesn't Heal the Way You Think

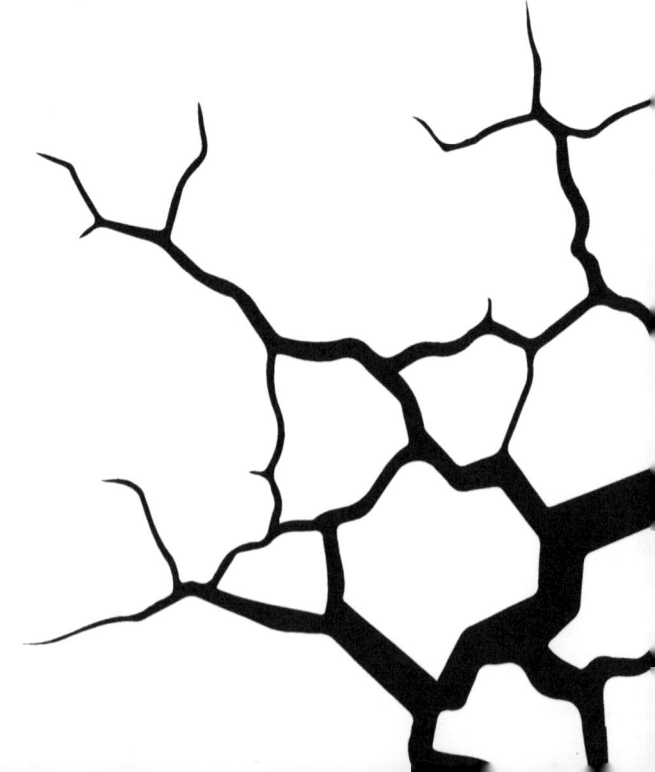

Grief doesn't work on a schedule. It works on a heartbeat.

Chapter 7

Take a breath, release the clock. Grief isn't measured in minutes—it's felt in moments. Let these questions sit with you:

Where have I felt pressured to "move on" before my heart was ready?

_____

_____

_____

_____

_____

_____

_____

_____

What does healing mean for me—does it mean forgetting, or carrying differently?

_____

_____

_____

_____

_____

_____

_____

_____

_____

_____

_____

Chapter 7 CONT.

These questions don't ask for deadlines—they ask for honesty.
Your pace is sacred. Your rhythm matters.

When has time felt like an ally, and when has it felt like a burden?

_____

_____

_____

_____

_____

_____

_____

_____

_____

How can I honor anniversaries, holidays, or ordinary days without
forcing myself into a timeline that isn't mine?

_____

_____

_____

_____

_____

_____

_____

_____

_____

_____

_____

NOTES & REFLECTIONS

Practical Anchors: Living Beyond the Calendar

- **Notice Your Rhythm** – Pay attention to when the waves hit. What stirs them? What soothes them?

- **Challenge the Pressure** – If someone asks, "Aren't you better yet?" try: "I'm moving at my own pace."

- **Ritualize Time** – Light a candle, cook their favorite meal, or mark anniversaries with intention. Rituals give grief a voice.

- **Give Yourself Permission** – Cry again. Laugh again. Remember again. None of it means you're "doing it wrong."

Notes 2 REMEMBER

CLOSING THOUGHT

SEVEN

Time alone doesn't heal.

What heals is the love you carry forward, the space you give yourself to feel, and the grace you extend to your own slow becoming.

Healing isn't about forgetting—it's about remembering with less fear. So if you're smiling today, let it be because you found a moment of light, not because you felt pressured to look "better."

Because true healing has never been about getting over. It's about learning to live within the rhythm of a changed life.

Not a deadline. A reshaping. Still whole. Still worthy. Still yours.

And just when you think you've found that rhythm, grief reminds you —it doesn't knock. It lets itself in. Uninvited, unannounced, slipping into the cracks of ordinary life.

That's where the next shadow begins.

A Self-Check Scale

The Unseen Weight: On a scale of 1 to 10, where would you place yourself on the balance of carrying your own grief versus your parent's?

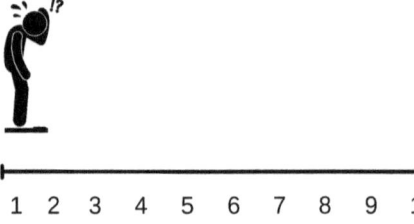

1 2 3 4 5 6 7 8 9 10

1: *I am actively holding space for my own grief while supporting my parent, and I feel a sense of emotional balance.*
10: *I feel completely consumed by my parent's grief, and my own feels heavy and invisible.*

My number today is: _____

Quite
REFLECTION

What emotion has been the loudest for you today

_____
_____
_____
_____
_____
_____
_____
_____
_____

*What detail
about your loved
one surfaced
today—a sound,
a phrase, a
habit?*

_____
_____
_____
_____

How did you show yourself grace, even in a small way?

_____
_____
_____
_____
_____
_____
_____
_____

NOTES & REFLECTIONS

Daily Check In

MOOD

WEATHER

DATE : _____

M T W T F S S

TODAY I FEEL

TODAY'S AFFIRMATION
-
-
-
-
-

TODAY'S MANTRA

TODAY I'M PROUD OF
-
-
-
-
-

TODAY'S MEMORY I CHOOSE TO CHERISH

TODAY'S GOAL
-
-
-
-
-

OPEN NOTES

TOMORROW'S PLAN
-
-
-
-

Chapter 8
When Grief Becomes the Uninvited Guest

66

What is grief, if not love persevering? – WandaVision

Chapter 8

Close your eyes. Picture the spaces they once filled—their chair, their laugh, their rituals. Then gently ask:

Where have I pressured myself to "get over" instead of learning to carry?

_____

_____

_____

_____

_____

_____

_____

_____

_____

What everyday places or objects still echo with their presence?

_____

_____

_____

_____

_____

_____

_____

_____

_____

_____

_____

_____

Chapter 8 CONT.

These aren't instructions for moving past. They're invitations to move with.

Which traditions feel too heavy to keep, and which ones could be tenderly rewritten?

_____

_____

_____

_____

_____

_____

_____

_____

_____

How might honoring their presence in the ordinary become a way of carrying them forward?

_____

_____

_____

_____

_____

_____

_____

_____

_____

_____

_____

NOTES & REFLECTIONS

Practical Anchors:
Moving With, Not Over

- **Allow the Echoes** – Notice what feels impossible right now. You don't have to rush back. Avoidance is not weakness; it's care.

- **Redefine Progress** – Smiling, laughing, or sharing a meal isn't betrayal. It's a reminder that humanity holds both ache and joy.

- **Honor Their Space** – Sit at their desk, walk their favorite path, or play their music. Let these be bridges, not barriers.

- **Gentle Scripts:**
  - **For yourself:** *"I can't face the porch today. That's okay."*
  - **For a parent:** *"We don't have to light the grill this year. Let's choose something gentler."*
  - **For siblings:** *"If the truck brings you closer to him, keep driving it. That's your way of carrying."*

Notes 2
REMEMBER

EIGHT
CLOSING THOUGHT

Grief never knocks. It barges in—through documents, through chairs and hats, through trucks that smell of cologne, through holidays that no longer feel the same.

It doesn't ask you to forget. It asks you to carry—with pauses, with substitutions, with whispers of "I'm not there yet."

Grief doesn't end. It lingers, it reshapes, it reminds.

And it reshapes not just you, but the whole family—because the same loss is carried in different languages.

NOTES & REFLECTIONS

_____
_____
_____
_____
_____
_____
_____
_____
_____
_____
_____
_____
_____
_____
_____

Quite
REFLECTION

What emotion has been the loudest for you today

_____
_____
_____
_____
_____
_____
_____
_____

What detail _____
about your loved _____
one surfaced _____
today—a sound, _____
a phrase, a _____
habit?

How did you show yourself grace, even in a small way?

_____
_____
_____
_____
_____
_____
_____
_____

NOTES & REFLECTIONS

Daily Check In

MOOD   ☺ ☹ 😑 😵 ☹

WEATHER   ☀ ☁ 🌬 🌧 ❄

DATE : _____

M   T   W   T   F   S   S

TODAY I FEEL

TODAY'S AFFIRMATION

-
-
-
-
-

TODAY'S MANTRA

TODAY I'M PROUD OF

-
-
-
-
-

TODAY'S MEMORY I CHOOSE TO CHERISH

TODAY'S GOAL

-
-
-
-
-

OPEN NOTES

TOMORROW'S PLAN

-
-
-
-

Chapter 9
When Family Grieves Differently

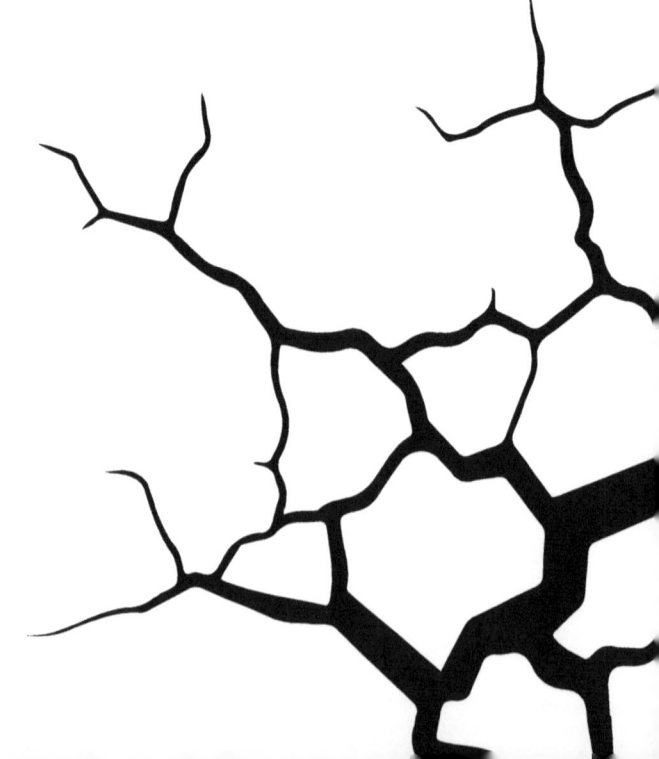

"

Same loss, different language.

Chapter 9

Take a steady breath. Let your shoulders drop. Then ask yourself gently:

REFLECTION: NAVIGATING GRIEF IN A FAMILY SYSTEM

Where do I notice differences in how my siblings or family members are grieving?

_____

_____

_____

_____

_____

_____

_____

_____

_____

How can I remind myself that "different" does not mean "less than"?

_____

_____

_____

_____

_____

_____

_____

_____

_____

_____

_____

Chapter 9 CONT.

These aren't questions to grade or solve. They're mirrors, catching you in the raw light of love and difference. Let them guide you toward patience—with your family, and with yourself.

What small step could I take to honor their way, even as I protect my own?

_____

_____

_____

_____

_____

_____

_____

_____

_____

Where might I need to ask for support—not to change how they grieve, but to share how I'm feeling?

_____

_____

_____

_____

_____

_____

_____

_____

_____

_____

_____

_____

Chapter 9 CONT.

What compassion can I extend to myself when their style feels far from mine?

_____

_____

_____

_____

_____

_____

_____

_____

_____

How might these differences reveal new strengths in our family, rather than only tensions?

_____

_____

_____

_____

_____

_____

_____

_____

_____

_____

_____

_____

NOTES & REFLECTIONS

Practical Anchors:
Navigating Family Grief

- **Recognize Roles:** Families fall into roles in grief—the planner, the comforter, the avoider, the over-functioner. None is "right" or "wrong." They're coping strategies.

- **Release Resentment:** Different doesn't mean absent. Even small gestures are contributions.

- **Draw Boundaries:** Protect your energy without demanding everyone grieve the same way.

- **Find Neutral Ground:** Choose activities or spaces where family can gather without pressure to grieve in unison.

Notes 2
REMEMBER

NINE

CLOSING THOUGHT

Grief isn't uniform. It wears many faces, many voices, many silences. Even in a shared loss, your grief remains distinctly yours.

And yet, when woven together, those different languages of sorrow can form something larger than conflict, they can form a chorus. Not always harmonious—sometimes jagged—but always proof that love endures.

Families don't survive by grieving the same way. They survive by listening for the love beneath each language, and choosing to stay at the table—even when the voices sound different.

Because the work isn't to grieve the same. The work is to grieve without fracturing.

A Self-Check Scale

The Unseen Weight: On a scale of 1 to 10, where would you place yourself on the balance of carrying your own grief versus your parent's?

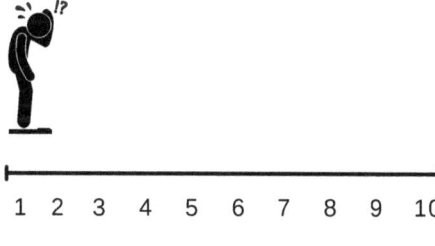

1 2 3 4 5 6 7 8 9 10

1: *I am actively holding space for my own grief while supporting my parent, and I feel a sense of emotional balance.*
10: *I feel completely consumed by my parent's grief, and my own feels heavy and invisible.*

My number today is: _____

Quite
REFLECTION

What emotion has been the loudest for you today

_____
_____
_____
_____
_____
_____
_____
_____

What detail
about your loved
one surfaced
today—a sound,
a phrase, a
habit?

_____
_____
_____
_____

How did you show yourself grace, even in a small way?

_____
_____
_____
_____
_____
_____
_____

Daily Check In

MOOD   😊 ☹️ 😑 😵 😫

WEATHER   ☀️ ☁️ 💨 🌦️ ❄️

DATE : _____

M   T   W   T   F   S   S

TODAY I FEEL

TODAY'S AFFIRMATION

-
-
-
-
-

TODAY'S MANTRA

TODAY I'M PROUD OF

-
-
-
-
-

TODAY'S MEMORY I CHOOSE TO CHERISH

TODAY'S GOAL

-
-
-
-
-

OPEN NOTES

TOMORROW'S PLAN

-
-
-
-

Chapter 10
Protecting Your Peace, No Apology Required

"

You don't owe anyone your depletion.

Chapter 10

Settle your shoulders. Let the air move slow. Then ask:

REFLECTION: WHERE CAN I MAKE SPACE FOR MYSELF?

Where in my life do I feel stretched past my true capacity?

_____

_____

_____

_____

_____

_____

_____

_____

_____

What have I been saying yes to out of guilt rather than alignment?

_____

_____

_____

_____

_____

_____

_____

_____

_____

_____

_____

Chapter 10 CONT.

These aren't rebellions. They're reminders: peace is a lifeline, not a luxury.

What boundary could I set this week that would feel like a breath of relief?

_____

_____

_____

_____

_____

_____

_____

_____

_____

What part of me needs permission to rest—without apology, without explanation?

_____

_____

_____

_____

_____

_____

_____

Who or what drains me most—and how might I step back, even a little, without shame?

_____

_____

_____

_____

_____

Chapter 10 CONT.

Practical Anchors:
Protecting Your Peace

- **Pause Before Yes:** Ask yourself, "Do I have the capacity for this?" before answering.
- **Soft Scripts:**
  - *"I want to help, but I don't have the space this week."*
  - *"I love you, and the answer is no for now."*

- **Use Delay as Protection:** *"Can I get back to you on that?"* buys time for honesty instead of reflexive yeses.

- **Choose Tender No's:** Declining with love (*"We'd love to see you, but not tonight"*) preserves relationships while guarding energy.

- **Treat Rest as Sacred:** Block time for yourself as if it were an appointment—with no apology.

Notes 2
REMEMBER

TEN

CLOSING THOUGHT

You are not selfish for needing space. You are not weak for saying no.

Every no you honor is a yes to your healing.

You don't have to be everything to everyone. Whole is enough. Whole is powerful. Whole is peace.

And as you practice this, you'll begin to notice something else: protecting your peace not only steadies you—it makes more room for your parent to begin rebuilding theirs.

Because protecting your peace is not just survival—*it's love.*

NOTES & REFLECTIONS

_____
_____
_____
_____
_____
_____
_____
_____
_____
_____
_____
_____
_____
_____
_____

NOTES & REFLECTIONS

NOTES & REFLECTIONS

Quite
REFLECTION

What emotion has been the loudest for you today

_____

_____

_____

_____

_____

_____

_____

_____

_____

What detail   _____
about your loved _____
one surfaced   _____
today—a sound, _____
a phrase, a
habit?   _____

How did you show yourself grace, even in a small way?

_____

_____

_____

_____

_____

_____

_____

_____

Daily Check In

MOOD

WEATHER

DATE : _____

M T W T F S S

TODAY I FEEL

TODAY'S AFFIRMATION

-
-
-
-
-

TODAY'S MANTRA

TODAY I'M PROUD OF

-
-
-
-
-

TODAY'S MEMORY I CHOOSE TO CHERISH

TODAY'S GOAL

-
-
-
-
-

OPEN NOTES

TOMORROW'S PLAN

-
-
-
-

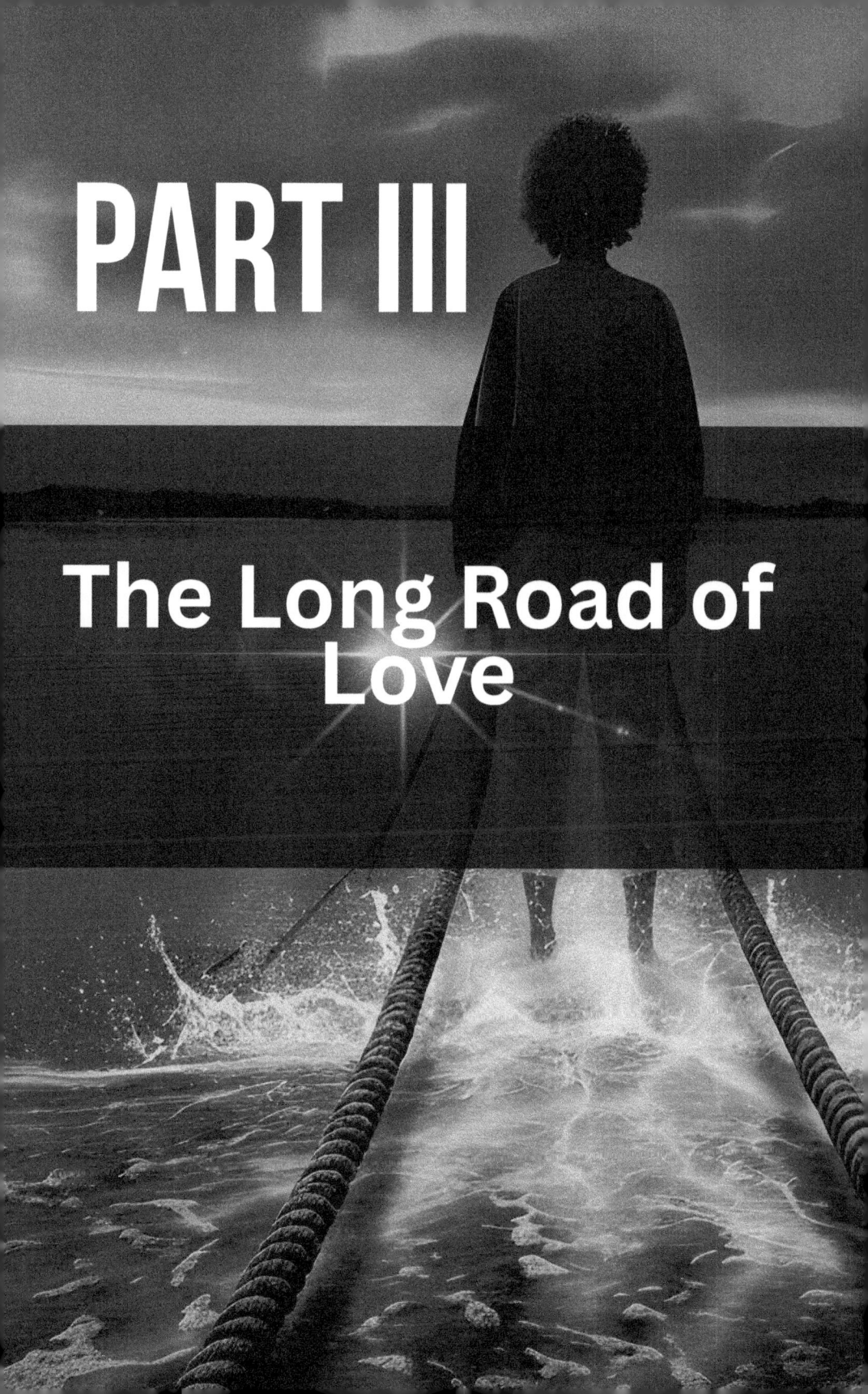

PART III

The Long Road of Love

NOTES & REFLECTIONS

NOTES & REFLECTIONS

Daily Check In

MOOD 😊 ☹️ 😐 😵 😖

WEATHER ☀️ ☁️ 🌬️ 🌧️ ❄️

DATE : _____

M T W T F S S

TODAY I FEEL

TODAY'S AFFIRMATION
-
-
-
-
-

TODAY'S MANTRA

TODAY I'M PROUD OF
-
-
-
-
-

TODAY'S MEMORY I CHOOSE TO CHERISH

TODAY'S GOAL
-
-
-
-
-

OPEN NOTES

TOMORROW'S PLAN
-
-
-
-

Chapter 11
Giving Yourself Permission to Be Okay

"

Healing doesn't mean forgetting. It means remembering without unraveling.

Chapter 11

Place your hand on your chest. Feel its rhythm. Then reflect:

Where have I been keeping life at a distance, afraid it would erase my grief?

_____

_____

_____

_____

_____

_____

_____

_____

_____

Where am I noticing sparks of lightness, even if fleeting?

_____

_____

_____

_____

_____

_____

_____

_____

_____

_____

Chapter 11 CONT.

These aren't signs of forgetting—they're gestures of grace, allowing life and love to weave together again.

How might joy coexist with memory, instead of competing with it?

_____

_____

_____

_____

_____

_____

_____

_____

Who in my circle makes space for both my sorrow and my laughter, without judgment?

_____

_____

_____

_____

_____

_____

What joy am I ready to allow back into my days without apology?

_____

_____

_____

_____

_____

_____

NOTES & REFLECTIONS

Practical Anchors:
Permission to Be Okay

- **Notice the Shift:** Pay attention when joy sneaks in—a smile, a rest, a laugh.

- **Challenge Guilt:** Replace "I shouldn't" with "I'm allowed."

- **Re-enter Slowly:** Let joy come in small steps.

- **Celebrate Ordinary:** Healing often shows up in everyday tasks—cooking, walking, resting.

- **Speak It Out Loud:** Tell someone about a joy you've allowed back in. Naming it makes it real.

Notes 2
REMEMBER

ELEVEN

CLOSING THOUGHT

There's no timeline for being okay—and no shame in arriving there.

Grief changes you, but it doesn't cancel your capacity for life.

Let the joy in—without apology. Let the light back through.
You don't have to prove your pain. You only have to honor your healing.

Being okay isn't forgetting—it's carrying love with more room for joy.

And when you give yourself that permission, you quietly give your parent permission too—to keep living, to keep becoming.

A Self-Check Scale

The Unseen Weight:
On a scale of 1 to 10,
where would you
place yourself on the
balance of carrying
your own grief versus
your parent's?

1 2 3 4 5 6 7 8 9 10

1: *I am actively holding space for my own grief while supporting my parent, and I feel a sense of emotional balance.*
10: *I feel completely consumed by my parent's grief, and my own feels heavy and invisible.*

My number today is: _____

Quite
REFLECTION

What emotion has been the loudest for you today

_____
_____
_____
_____
_____
_____
_____
_____

What detail _____
about your loved _____
one surfaced _____
today—a sound, _____
a phrase, a
habit?

How did you show yourself grace, even in a small way?

_____
_____
_____
_____
_____
_____
_____

NOTES & REFLECTIONS

Daily Check In

MOOD   ☺ ☹ 😑 😵 🙁

WEATHER   ☀ ☁ 🌬 🌧 ❄

DATE : _____

M   T   W   T   F   S   S

TODAY I FEEL

TODAY'S AFFIRMATION

-
-
-
-
-

TODAY'S MANTRA

TODAY I'M PROUD OF

-
-
-
-
-

TODAY'S MEMORY I CHOOSE TO CHERISH

TODAY'S GOAL

-
-
-
-
-

OPEN NOTES

TOMORROW'S PLAN

-
-
-
-

Chapter 12
Witnessing the Becoming

> We mourn who they were, even as we walk beside who they are becoming.

Chapter 12

Take a steadying breath. Settle into the stillness. Let these questions open gently, like doors you don't have to rush through:

What parts of my parent feel unfamiliar now—and how might they be signs of who they are becoming, rather than only what's been lost?

_____

_____

_____

_____

_____

_____

_____

_____

_____

Where do I catch glimpses of resilience, even if small—an everyday act that hints at their strength returning?

_____

_____

_____

_____

_____

_____

_____

_____

_____

_____

_____

_____

Chapter 12 CONT.

These aren't questions to fix. They are invitations—to notice, to soften, to expand the lens through which you see both your parent and yourself. Grief reshapes slowly. The witnessing is part of the love.

How can I stand beside them in ways that steady, but do not control?

_____

_____

_____

_____

_____

_____

_____

_____

_____

What version of them am I clinging to—and what would it mean to release that version while still honoring their essence?

_____

_____

_____

_____

_____

_____

_____

_____

_____

_____

_____

NOTES & REFLECTIONS

Practical Anchors:
Walking Beside the Becoming

- **Notice Without Forcing:** Observe shifts in your parent's energy, routines, or moods without pressuring them to "return" to their old self.
- **Honor the Still Days:** Quiet isn't a setback—it's part of the rhythm of rebuilding. Stillness holds its own kind of strength.
- **Encourage Gently:** Offer invitations, not ultimatums. "Would you like me to join you for a walk?" carries more grace than "You should get out more."
- **Celebrate Small Restorations:** Making coffee, attending a tournament, volunteering at a playhouse, acknowledge these as victories, however ordinary they may seem.

Notes 2
REMEMBER

CLOSING THOUGHT

TWELVE

Your parent's grief will reshape them, but it does not erase them.

Hold space for who they were. Hold hope for who they are becoming.

Because love doesn't cling only to the past—it also sows seeds for the future.

(pause)

And sometimes, the greatest gift you can give is not to demand the return of who they once were, but to stand beside them long enough to watch who they are becoming.

_____

_____

_____

_____

_____

_____

_____

_____

_____

_____

_____

_____

_____

_____

_____

Quite
REFLECTION

What emotion has been the loudest for you today

_____

_____

_____

_____

_____

_____

_____

_____

_____

What detail
about your loved
one surfaced
today—a sound,
a phrase, a
habit?

_____

_____

_____

_____

How did you show yourself grace, even in a small way?

_____

_____

_____

_____

_____

_____

_____

_____

NOTES & REFLECTIONS

Daily Check In

MOOD   😊 😦 😑 😵 😟

WEATHER   ☀️ ☁️ 💨 🌧️ ❄️

DATE : _____

M   T   W   T   F   S   S

TODAY I FEEL

TODAY'S AFFIRMATION

-
-
-
-
-

TODAY'S MANTRA

TODAY I'M PROUD OF

-
-
-
-
-

TODAY'S MEMORY I CHOOSE TO CHERISH

TODAY'S GOAL

-
-
-
-
-

OPEN NOTES

TOMORROW'S PLAN

-
-
-
-

Chapter 13

When the Support Ends and the Silence Echoes

> **The Cards Stop. The Calls Fade. And Suddenly, It's Just You and the Quiet.**

Chapter 13

Take a breath. Let the quiet around you settle. Then reflect slowly:

Where do I feel the deepest silence—in my home, my relationships, or within myself?

_____
_____
_____
_____
_____
_____
_____
_____
_____

When support faded, what did I miss most: the practical help, the conversations, or simply the reminder that others remembered I was still grieving?

_____
_____
_____
_____
_____
_____
_____
_____
_____
_____
_____
_____

Chapter 13 CONT.

These aren't questions to fix overnight. They are pathways back to remembering that even in silence, your story—and your needs—still matter.

Who in my circle can I be honest with about my ongoing grief—and what would it look like to invite them back into my support system?

_____

_____

_____

_____

_____

_____

_____

_____

_____

What request for support have I been afraid to make—and what might change if I voiced it gently?

_____

_____

_____

_____

_____

_____

_____

_____

_____

_____

Chapter 13 CONT.

How do I care for myself when others are not present—what rituals, spaces, or practices remind me I am still held?

_____

_____

_____

_____

_____

_____

_____

_____

_____

_____

How can I learn to see silence not only as emptiness, but also as space for rest, memory, or renewal?

_____

_____

_____

_____

_____

_____

_____

_____

_____

_____

NOTES & REFLECTIONS

Rebuilding Support on Your Terms

- **Letting one trusted person know:** *"I'm still not okay."*

- **Starting a small ritual** to honor your loved one.

- **Joining a grief group** or faith community.

- **Writing, creating, or walking** as forms of release.

- **Asking siblings, friends, or family** for specific commitments: a weekly call, a dinner, a shared check-in.

- **Gently reminding others:** "My grief didn't end when the funeral did."

- **Support may not look like it did in the beginning**—but that doesn't mean it's gone.

Notes 2
REMEMBER

THIRTEEN

CLOSING THOUGHT

The silence may feel hollow—but it is also space.

Space for remembering. Space for release. Space for rebuilding.

That floral queen chair became more than a seat for my mother. It became a reminder that even in quiet, there is presence. Even in stillness, there is story.

The world may grow quiet around you, but you are not forgotten. You are still held—in memory, in community, and in love that continues forward.

In time, we would each return to our own rhythms—me to my home, my mother to her quiet rituals—but in those early months, we were still learning how to let the silence hold us, together.

A Self-Check Scale

The Unseen Weight: On a scale of 1 to 10, where would you place yourself on the balance of carrying your own grief versus your parent's?

1 2 3 4 5 6 7 8 9 10

1: *I am actively holding space for my own grief while supporting my parent, and I feel a sense of emotional balance.*
10: *I feel completely consumed by my parent's grief, and my own feels heavy and invisible.*

My number today is: _____

Quite REFLECTION

What emotion has been the loudest for you today

_____

_____

_____

_____

_____

_____

_____

_____

_____

What detail about your loved one surfaced today—a sound, a phrase, a habit?

_____

_____

_____

_____

_____

How did you show yourself grace, even in a small way?

_____

_____

_____

_____

_____

_____

_____

_____

NOTES & REFLECTIONS

Daily Check In

MOOD ☺ ☹ 😑 😵 ☹

WEATHER ☀ ☁ 🌬 🌧 ❄

DATE : _____

M T W T F S S

TODAY I FEEL

TODAY'S AFFIRMATION

- ●
- ●
- ●
- ●
- ●

TODAY'S MANTRA

TODAY I'M PROUD OF

- ●
- ●
- ●
- ●
- ●

TODAY'S MEMORY I CHOOSE TO CHERISH

TODAY'S GOAL

- ●
- ●
- ●
- ●
- ●

OPEN NOTES

TOMORROW'S PLAN

- ●
- ●
- ●
- ●

Chapter 14

When their Absence Meets Your Milestones

The celebration doesn't erase the sorrow—it carries it.

Chapter 14

Settle your shoulders. Breathe slow. Then let these questions meet you where you are:

If they were here, how would they have celebrated me—what words, what gestures, what presence?

_____

_____

_____

_____

_____

_____

_____

_____

Where can I honor that spirit in my own way? A candle? A toast? A whispered thank you?

_____

_____

_____

_____

_____

_____

_____

_____

_____

_____

Chapter 14 CONT.

These aren't assignments to check off. They are invitations—to carry both absence and presence into the life that keeps unfolding.

What permission do I need to give myself—to feel joy, to laugh, to plan—without guilt?

_____

_____

_____

_____

_____

_____

_____

_____

How might I invite others into remembering, so I don't carry the silence alone?

_____

_____

_____

_____

_____

_____

_____

What tradition could I begin now, one that honors them each time a milestone arrives, so love has a place to land?

_____

_____

_____

_____

_____

_____

NOTES & REFLECTIONS

Practical Anchors:
Carrying Them Into Your Milestones

- **Mark the Day:** Create a ritual when milestones arrive—a prayer, a toast, a candle, a story.

- **Share Their Legacy:** Invite others to name a favorite memory at the gathering.

- **Carry a Token:** Wear their jewelry, carry their handkerchief, slip a note in your pocket.

- **Blend Joy and Grief:** Let yourself cry and celebrate. Both belong.

- **Choose Continuity:** Keep one tradition they loved, while starting a new one that reflects life now.

- **Gentle Script:** Whisper to yourself, *"I wish you were here. I'm carrying you with me today."*

Notes 2 REMEMBER

FOURTEEN

CLOSING THOUGHT

You're allowed to feel it all. To cry and dance. To miss them and celebrate yourself.

Their absence may echo. But your joy still matters.

Because love, even after loss, finds its way into every milestone you reach. Like those pink roses, it may change form, but it will keep blooming—quietly, steadily, against all odds.

The silence that once held only ache now holds remembrance.

And when you allow space for both, you honor not only their memory but also your own becoming.

_____
_____
_____
_____
_____
_____
_____
_____
_____
_____
_____
_____
_____
_____
_____

Quite
REFLECTION

What emotion has been the loudest for you today

_____
_____
_____
_____
_____
_____
_____
_____
_____

What detail about your loved one surfaced today—a sound, a phrase, a habit?

_____
_____
_____
_____
_____

How did you show yourself grace, even in a small way?

_____
_____
_____
_____
_____
_____
_____
_____

NOTES & REFLECTIONS

Daily Check In

MOOD ☺ ☹ 😑 😵 😖

WEATHER ☀ ☁ 💨 🌧 ❄

DATE : _____

M T W T F S S

TODAY I FEEL

TODAY'S AFFIRMATION
-
-
-
-
-

TODAY'S MANTRA

TODAY I'M PROUD OF
-
-
-
-
-

TODAY'S MEMORY I CHOOSE TO CHERISH

TODAY'S GOAL
-
-
-
-
-

OPEN NOTES

TOMORROW'S PLAN
-
-
-
-

Chapter 15

What Moving on Really Looks Like

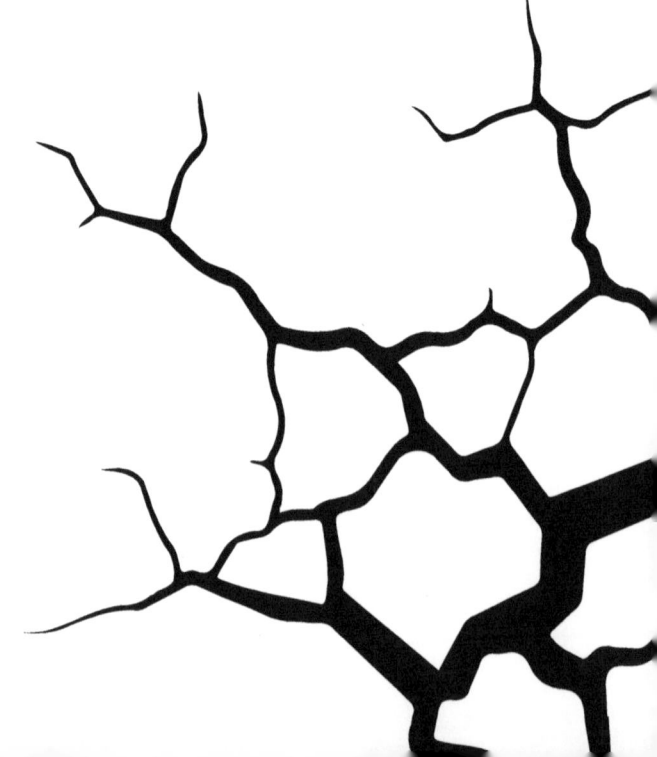

"

You don't move on. You move forward—with what remains.

Chapter 15

Take a breath. Feel your feet steady against the floor. Let these questions open softly:

What messages about "moving on" have I absorbed—from culture, family, or community—that don't fit my reality?

_____

_____

_____

_____

_____

_____

_____

_____

_____

In what small ways has grief changed me—and how can I honor that growth instead of fearing it?

_____

_____

_____

_____

_____

_____

_____

_____

_____

_____

_____

_____

Chapter 15 CONT.

These aren't assignments to check off. They are invitations—to carry both absence and presence into the life that keeps unfolding.

What part of my life am I ready to reimagine, not erase?

_____

_____

_____

_____

_____

_____

_____

How do I want to carry their presence into new milestones or seasons ahead?

_____

_____

_____

_____

_____

_____

What does "forward" mean to me today—and how might that meaning change tomorrow?

_____

_____

_____

_____

_____

NOTES & REFLECTIONS

Practical Anchors: Living Forward Without Leaving Behind

- **Name the Growth:** Notice one part of yourself that has expanded since the loss—resilience, empathy, patience.

- **Mark Gentle Firsts:** A first holiday, trip, or gathering can feel raw. Choose one ritual to honor their presence while embracing your new experience.

- **Honor the Return of Tears:** Tears after months of progress aren't regressions; they're reminders that love still lives.

- **Invite Life In:** Say yes to something small—a walk, a project, a dinner. Let life return without demanding it erase grief.

- **Carry Tokens:** A phrase, photo, or tradition can travel with you into new spaces. You don't leave them—you bring them.

- **Share Your Language:** Tell someone close: "Forward doesn't mean I'm over it—it means I'm carrying them as I go."

Notes 2
REMEMBER

FIFTEEN

CLOSING THOUGHT

You don't have to move on.

You only have to move honestly.

With your grief. With your growth. With your memories.

You're still becoming. And that, too, is love.

And as you move forward, you show your parent—and yourself—that healing isn't leaving. It's carrying.

A Self-Check Scale

The Unseen Weight: On a scale of 1 to 10, where would you place yourself on the balance of carrying your own grief versus your parent's?

1 2 3 4 5 6 7 8 9 10

1: *I am actively holding space for my own grief while supporting my parent, and I feel a sense of emotional balance.*
10: *I feel completely consumed by my parent's grief, and my own feels heavy and invisible.*

My number today is: _____

_____

_____

_____

_____

_____

_____

Quite
REFLECTION

What emotion has been the loudest for you today

_____
_____
_____
_____
_____
_____
_____
_____
_____

What detail
about your loved
one surfaced
today—a sound,
a phrase, a
habit?

_____
_____
_____
_____

How did you show yourself grace, even in a small way?

_____
_____
_____
_____
_____
_____
_____
_____

NOTES & REFLECTIONS

Daily Check In

MOOD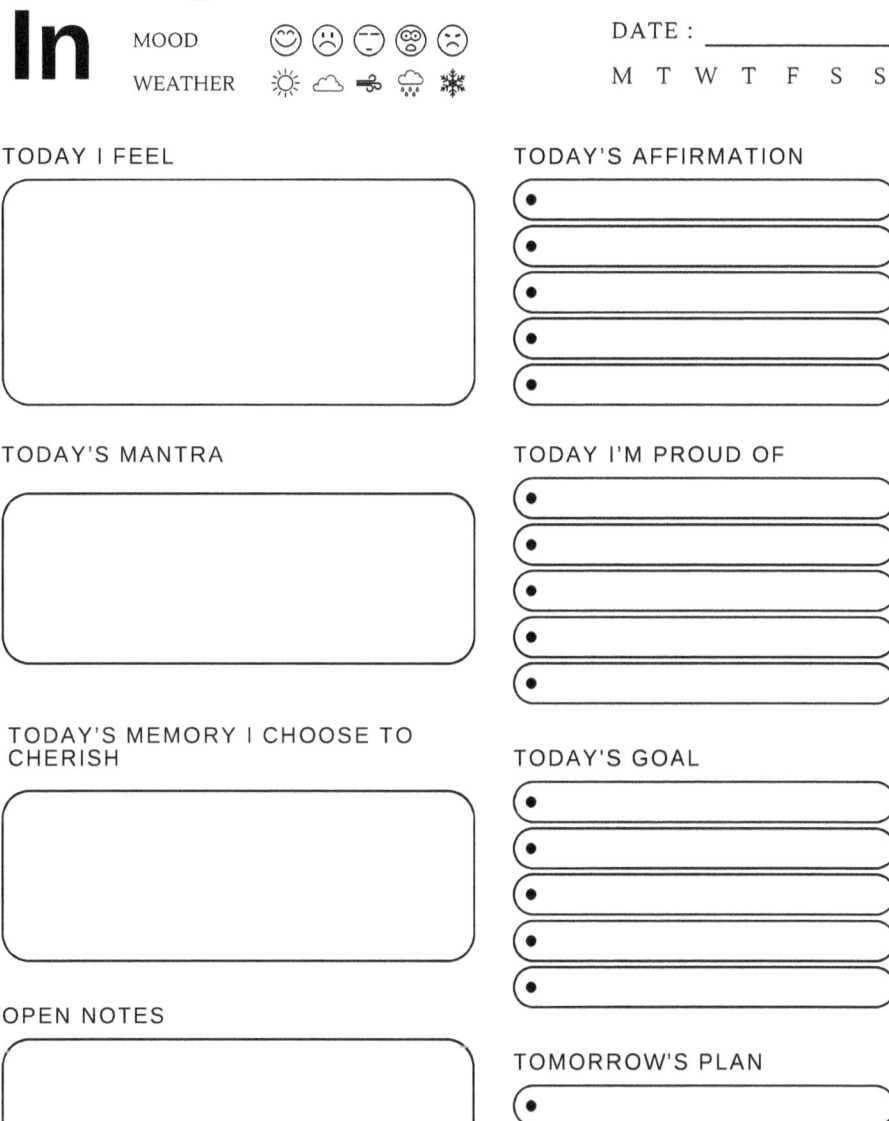

WEATHER

DATE : _____

M T W T F S S

TODAY I FEEL

TODAY'S AFFIRMATION

-
-
-
-
-

TODAY'S MANTRA

TODAY I'M PROUD OF

-
-
-
-
-

TODAY'S MEMORY I CHOOSE TO CHERISH

TODAY'S GOAL

-
-
-
-
-

OPEN NOTES

TOMORROW'S PLAN

-
-
-
-

Chapter 16
The Role you Never Asked For

66

I didn't choose this role. But I can choose how I carry it.

Chapter 16

Take a breath. Place your hand on your chest. Ask yourself gently:

What role did I step into after the loss that I never asked for?

_____

_____

_____

_____

_____

_____

_____

_____

Which of those responsibilities feel heavy—and which feel meaningful?

_____

_____

_____

_____

_____

_____

Where have I been carrying out of fear, guilt, or expectation rather than love?

_____

_____

_____

_____

_____

Chapter 16

These aren't questions of blame. They are questions of balance—reminders that you're not only a caretaker, but also a human being with needs of your own.

Who can I invite to share one small piece of this load?

_____

_____

_____

_____

_____

_____

_____

_____

How might I honor my parent while still protecting my own becoming?

_____

_____

_____

_____

_____

_____

_____

In what ways have I become the "parent" in moments where I used to be the child—and how do I feel about that shift?

_____

_____

_____

_____

_____

_____

NOTES & REFLECTIONS

Choosing Agency in
the Unchosen

- **Name It:** Say out loud, "I didn't choose this, but I am choosing how I respond." Naming breaks the illusion that duty is destiny.

- **Share It:** Invite siblings, cousins, or close friends to carry pieces with you. A check-in call, a grocery run, or simply visiting can redistribute the weight.

- **Redefine It:** You're not your parent's savior. You're their support. That distinction frees you from impossible expectations.

- **Release It:** Some responsibilities don't belong to you. Hand back what isn't yours, even if it feels awkward.

- **Communicate Clearly:** Tell your parent gently, *"I'll help with this part, but I can't do everything."* Boundaries are not abandonment—they are honesty.

Notes 2
REMEMBER

SIXTEEN

CLOSING THOUGHT

The role you never asked for may never feel natural.
But it doesn't have to undo you.

You can carry it differently. With limits. With honesty.
With a posture that says: "I am here, but I am still me."

Because love doesn't demand your depletion.
It only asks for your presence.

And sometimes, the greatest gift you can give your parent isn't
perfection—it's the courage to stand beside them without losing
yourself in the process.

_____
_____
_____
_____
_____
_____
_____
_____
_____
_____
_____
_____
_____
_____
_____
_____

Quite REFLECTION

What emotion has been the loudest for you today

_____
_____
_____
_____
_____
_____
_____
_____
_____

What detail _____
about your loved _____
one surfaced _____
today—a sound, _____
a phrase, a _____
habit?

How did you show yourself grace, even in a small way?

_____
_____
_____
_____
_____
_____
_____
_____

NOTES & REFLECTIONS

Daily Check In

TODAY I FEEL

TODAY'S AFFIRMATION

-
-
-
-
-

TODAY'S MANTRA

TODAY I'M PROUD OF

-
-
-
-
-

TODAY'S MEMORY I CHOOSE TO CHERISH

TODAY'S GOAL

-
-
-
-
-

OPEN NOTES

TOMORROW'S PLAN

-
-
-
-

Chapter 17
What Grief Taught Me About Love

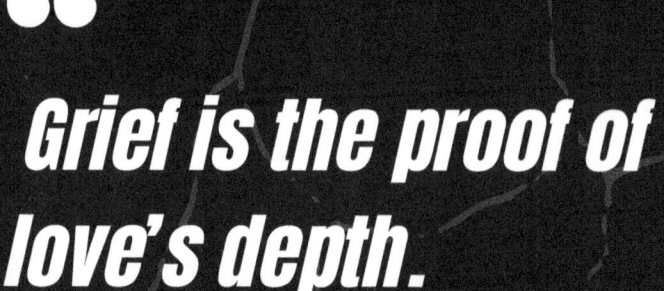

Grief is the proof of love's depth.

Chapter 17

Take a steady breath. Let your shoulders drop. Then ask yourself gently:

Where has grief revealed just how deeply I loved?

_____

_____

_____

_____

_____

_____

_____

_____

What everyday spaces, objects, or moments still carry their presence?

_____

_____

_____

_____

_____

_____

How has my love shifted form—showing up now in care for my parent, or tenderness toward myself?

_____

_____

_____

_____

Chapter 17 CONT.

These aren't demands for answers. They're invitations—to notice how love, even in grief, keeps reshaping you: quietly, steadily, endlessly.

When has grief expanded my capacity to love others more fully, even in small ways?

_____

_____

_____

_____

_____

_____

_____

_____

_____

_____

_____

What pieces of their love do I long to carry forward into my own story and legacy?

_____

_____

_____

_____

_____

_____

_____

_____

_____

_____

_____

_____

NOTES & REFLECTIONS

Practical Anchors:
Letting Love Lead the Grief

- **Name the Love Beneath the Ache:** When the tears come, whisper: This hurts because I loved deeply.

- **Notice the Fingerprints:** Write down the quirks, habits, or sayings that still surface. These are love's echoes.

- **Practice Love-in-Action:** Cook a recipe, play their song, teach a child something they once taught you.

- **Expand Love's Reach:** Let grief soften your compassion toward others.

- **Reframe the Weight:** Instead of asking When will this grief end? try How is love still alive in me through this grief?

Notes 2
REMEMBER

SEVENTEEN

CLOSING THOUGHT

Grief is not love's opposite. It is love's proof.

Every ache, every tear, every pause in the middle of the day is evidence that what you shared mattered—and still does.

What grief taught me about love is simple, but profound:
Love does not end. It reshapes. It lingers. It carries us forward.

Though the ache remains, so does the love.

And in the end, it's love that keeps you steady enough to carry the grief—the one thing strong enough to hold both memory and becoming.

A Self-Check Scale

The Unseen Weight: On a scale of 1 to 10, where would you place yourself on the balance of carrying your own grief versus your parent's?

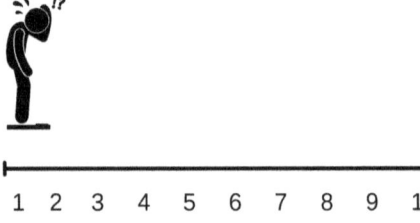

1 2 3 4 5 6 7 8 9 10

1: *I am actively holding space for my own grief while supporting my parent, and I feel a sense of emotional balance.*
10: *I feel completely consumed by my parent's grief, and my own feels heavy and invisible.*

My number today is: _____

Quite
REFLECTION

What emotion has been the loudest for you today

_____
_____
_____
_____
_____
_____
_____
_____
_____

What detail _____
about your loved _____
one surfaced _____
today—a sound, _____
a phrase, a _____
habit?

How did you show yourself grace, even in a small way?

_____
_____
_____
_____
_____
_____
_____
_____

NOTES & REFLECTIONS

Daily Check In

MOOD   😊 😞 😑 😵 😣

WEATHER   ☀️ ☁️ 🌬️ 🌧️ ❄️

DATE : _____

M   T   W   T   F   S   S

TODAY I FEEL

TODAY'S AFFIRMATION

-
-
-
-
-

TODAY'S MANTRA

TODAY I'M PROUD OF

-
-
-
-
-

TODAY'S MEMORY I CHOOSE TO CHERISH

TODAY'S GOAL

-
-
-
-
-

OPEN NOTES

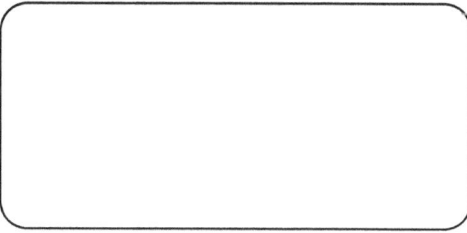

TOMORROW'S PLAN

-
-
-
-

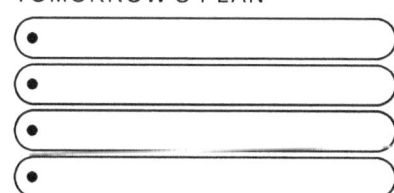

Chapter 18
Life After the Breaking Point

Grief is not just an emotion; it's a to-do list." - Unknown

Chapter 18

Take a breath. Reflect:

What do I want to bring with me from this season of grief?

_____

_____

_____

_____

_____

_____

_____

_____

_____

_____

_____

What no longer serves me in this new chapter?

_____

_____

_____

_____

_____

_____

_____

_____

_____

_____

_____

Chapter 18 CONT.

How has loss shaped my view of life and love?

_____

_____

_____

_____

_____

_____

_____

_____

_____

_____

_____

_____

_____

What does rebuilding mean to me now?

_____

_____

_____

_____

_____

_____

_____

_____

_____

_____

_____

_____

NOTES & REFLECTIONS

CLOSING THOUGHT

The journey doesn't end here. It continues—in the way you live, love, and remember.

Grief may have changed you. But it hasn't broken you.

You're still here. Still loving. Still becoming. And your life—though shaped by loss—is still rich with meaning, possibility, and love.

You have walked through fire, and you are still standing.
That is your proof—
 you are already holding without breaking.

A Self-Check Scale

The Unseen Weight: On a scale of 1 to 10, where would you place yourself on the balance of carrying your own grief versus your parent's?

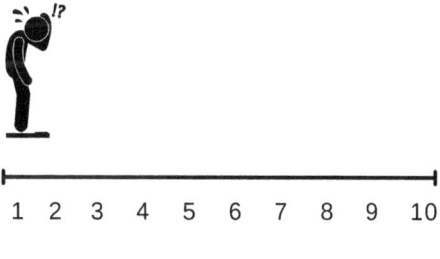

1 2 3 4 5 6 7 8 9 10

1: *I am actively holding space for my own grief while supporting my parent, and I feel a sense of emotional balance.*
10: *I feel completely consumed by my parent's grief, and my own feels heavy and invisible.*

My number today is: _____

NOTES & REFLECTIONS

Quite
REFLECTION

What emotion has been the loudest for you today

_____
_____
_____
_____
_____
_____
_____
_____
_____

*What detail
about your loved
one surfaced
today—a sound,
a phrase, a
habit?*

_____
_____
_____
_____

How did you show yourself grace, even in a small way?

_____
_____
_____
_____
_____
_____
_____

NOTES & REFLECTIONS

Daily Check In

MOOD 😊 😟 😑 😵 😣

WEATHER ☀ ☁ 🌬 🌧 ❄

TODAY I FEEL

TODAY'S AFFIRMATION

- ●
- ●
- ●
- ●
- ●

TODAY'S MANTRA

TODAY I'M PROUD OF

- ●
- ●
- ●
- ●
- ●

TODAY'S MEMORY I CHOOSE TO CHERISH

TODAY'S GOAL

- ●
- ●
- ●
- ●
- ●

OPEN NOTES

TOMORROW'S PLAN

- ●
- ●
- ●
- ●

Bonus Reflection

Anchors for the Road Ahead: The Four Pillars That Hold You Steady

Supporting a grieving parent doesn't mean losing yourself in the process. It means learning how to stand beside them—without disappearing.

Bonus Chapter

Pause. Place your hand over your heart. Then ask yourself:

Where do I see their love still alive in my daily life?

_____

_____

_____

_____

_____

_____

_____

_____

_____

_____

_____

_____

What new joys, however small, am I ready to let in—without guilt, without apology?

_____

_____

_____

_____

_____

_____

_____

_____

_____

_____

_____

_____

Bonus Chapter CONT.

How has grief changed the way I show up for love—with my parent and with myself?

_____

_____

_____

_____

_____

_____

_____

_____

_____

_____

_____

_____

_____

In what ways can I carry their presence forward—through rituals, stories, or the life I'm still shaping?

_____

_____

_____

_____

_____

_____

_____

_____

_____

_____

_____

_____

NOTES & REFLECTIONS

NOTES & REFLECTIONS

Tips for Navigating
The Unknown

- **Make Lists:** Write down tasks, but circle only what must happen this week.

- **Do It Together:** Sit with your parent during calls, even if they don't say much.

- **Build Breaks In:** After an hour of paperwork, step outside and breathe.

- **Delegate Wisely:** *"I'll handle Social Security, but could you take utilities? Sharing the load will help us all breathe."*

Notes 2
REMEMBER

Quite
REFLECTION

What emotion has been the loudest for you today

_____
_____
_____
_____
_____
_____
_____
_____
_____

What detail _____
about your loved _____
one surfaced _____
today—a sound, _____
a phrase, a _____
habit?

How did you show yourself grace, even in a small way?

_____
_____
_____
_____
_____
_____
_____
_____

NOTES & REFLECTIONS

NOTES & REFLECTIONS

NOTES & REFLECTIONS

Daily Check In

MOOD   ☺ ☹ 😌 😵 😖

WEATHER   ☀ ☁ 💨 🌧 ❄

DATE : _____

M   T   W   T   F   S   S

TODAY I FEEL

TODAY'S AFFIRMATION
-
-
-
-
-

TODAY'S MANTRA

TODAY I'M PROUD OF
-
-
-
-
-

TODAY'S MEMORY I CHOOSE TO CHERISH

TODAY'S GOAL
-
-
-
-
-

OPEN NOTES

TOMORROW'S PLAN
-
-
-
-

Love Unbroken

Steady

EVOLVE

RESILIENCE

BOUNDARIES

Bloom

RESILIENCE

WALKING

Reclaim Strength

LAYERS

Moving With

YOUR HEALING
MATTERS TOO

Healing

HOLD SPACE FOR
YOUR OWN HEART

Sanctuary

BECOMING

RESILIENCE   TRUST THE PROCESS

VITAL

REBUILDING

YOU ARE ENOUGH.

HEALING HAPPENS IN COMMUNITY

Seen

A Note From Mischere

Thank you for trusting this space, and yourself, enough to fill it.

My hope is that this companion journal has been more than a tool. I hope it's been a quiet place where you could breathe, feel, and begin to release.
As you close these pages, remember: healing isn't a destination. It's a rhythm —of holding, loosening, and beginning again.

With care and gratitude,

Mischere V. Kyles
Author of Holding Without Breaking
Creator of the Lineage & Legacy Collection

Lineage & Legacy
Publishing

www.ingramcontent.com/pod-product-compliance
Lightning Source LLC
Chambersburg PA
CBHW050446150626
46551CB00029B/1832